More Parables Lite

Twelve Parables of Jesus and a Gospel Story retold for two voices

Mike Stone

kevin
mayhew

First published in 2003 by

KEVIN MAYHEW LTD
Buxhall, Stowmarket, Suffolk, IP14 3BW
E-mail: info@kevinmayhewltd.com

KINGSGATE PUBLISHING INC
1000 Pannell Street, Suite G, Columbia, MO 65201
E-mail: sales@kingsgatepublishing.com

9 8 7 6 5 4 3 2 1 0

ISBN 1 84417 157 4
Catalogue No 1500645

Front cover design by Angela Selfe
Edited by Graham Harris
Typesetting by Louise Selfe
Printed and bound in Great Britain

Contents

About the author

During a professional career in computer software, Mike Stone served his parish church as Reader and Non-stipendiary Priest. Retiring from these, he found activity working in a Christian bookshop, and has occasional opportunities of ministry in church and a pastoral concern among the elderly. He has nearly always seen the funny – even peculiar – side of church and Christian life.

His first collection of stories in this dialogue style, *Parables Lite*, is also published by Kevin Mayhew. Other published works include *Introductions to the Lessons* (Columba, 2000), material widely used in churches which follow the Common Worship Lectionary.

Introduction

This book contains twelve Gospel parables and one Gospel story, retold in a dialogue form to be read out loud.

In these pieces, as in my previous collection, *Parables Lite*, I have let my imagination run wild on some of the parables of Jesus in the Gospels. The purpose in these retellings of well-known stories is to make them fresh and appealing to today's hearers – just as once they made their mark on those who listened to Jesus. So I give them new settings, often thoroughly anachronistic. And the dialogues are packed with the kind of verbal gymnastics many of my friends (and congregations) share, enjoy, and laugh at.

'The way to a man's heart is through his . . . *funny-bone.'* Fanny Fern wrote 'stomach', but I'm not going for belly-laughs. Gentle humour must surely have been part of Jesus' storytelling technique, and in these dialogues you will find enough to generate some chuckles and smiles. This kind of fun presentation touches hearts as deeply as any serious sermon.

There is, of course, always a serious point and lesson in every one of Jesus' stories, and I hope to remain faithful to that, while reflecting on them in much the way the young church reflected on them and found truths for themselves in their situations.

And for those who want their faith to be taken very seriously at all times, I recommend a line from that superb Christian poet and playwright Christopher Fry, who loves to play with the sounds and senses of words: 'Laughter is surely/The surest touch of genius in creation' (*The Lady's Not for Burning*).

Green grow the dandelions

1   G'day

2   G'day, sport

1   Sports and games

2   Were popular in Palestine

1   So when Jesus told stories about farms and fields

2   He could have said sports fields and stadiums

1   Perhaps he did

2   People would have understood

1   Greek culture was popular

2   Greek language

1   Greek restaurants

2   Greek athletics

1   There were gymnasiums and sports stadiums everywhere

2   Even in Gasera

1   Far up in the North-East

2   Near the source of the Jordan

1   Where the people were called Jord['n]ese

2   Now although there were some pious Palestinian puritanical spoilsports

1   Most Jews liked a day at the races

2   Horse races

1   Mixed races

2   Human races

1   Great crowds at the stadiums

2   Ticket touts

1   Nearly-new refreshments

2   Locusts on sticks and honeybuns

1   Grass tracks for the athletics

2   The men always ran without T-shirts

1   No Y-fronts

2   Or G-strings

1   Or J-cloths

2   Which was a sight for sore feet

1   And the female mud wrestlers

2   Were always popular

     PAUSE

1   Now Herod

2   That's *not* the Herod who lost his way with Pilate

1   But his father

2   Herod the Great

1   The one who was grandiose, bellicose and otiose

2   The one who failed his audition for the Bethlehem Samaritans

1   He was always building things

2   Temples, palaces, theatres

1   Entire cities in Greek style

2   Herod liked games

1   Especially indoor games

2   Mixed doubles

1   With his twelve wives

2   But he also appeared at big sporting events in the royal box

1   In his royal leathers covered with royal chains

2   Torture-Chambers 'R' Us

1   So, when Jesus told a kingdom story

2   About how seeds and weeds grow, good and bad together

1   Until God's harvest

2   Jesus *could* have said:

1   You remember how Herod initiated the Quinquennial Games

2   To rival the Olympics and the Isthmians

1   And had an immaculate conception

2   For the new national stadium in Jerusalem

1   Which is built right next door to the Temple

2   (That's absolutely true!)

1   Twin towers and designer changing-rooms

2   Twin tracks and designer standing-room

1   A vast site

2   No expanse spared

1   Expensive turf for the track

2   From the famous gardener designer

1   Risibility Green

2   The Laughing Lawn-Layer

1   A man of many parts

2   Most of which were not in the catalogue

1   Was that really his own name?

2   Well, no one had asked for it back

1   He laid the running track with care

2   Guaranteed personal knees-on service

1   Quick-growing grass

2   Plant and stand back

1   Kept it watered through the ducts

2   Kept the ducks off the water

1   Grow and mow

2   Mow and grow

1   Took up a lot of time

2   It's a non-renewable resource

PAUSE

1   Three weeks later

2   Risibility Green was standing at the trackside

1   Saw the grass was greener on the other side

2   And no wonder

1   Calamity!

2   Disaster!

1   A riot of daisies

2   Dandelions and buttercups

1   And a swarm of bees

2   Composing a Pollenaise

1   You couldn't see the good grass

2   For the weeds

1   Green reported the sight to the site manager

2   Who saw what had happened

1   Green weed seeds had been mixed with lovely lawn

2   In the grass-hopper

1   Moan and groan

2   Groan and moan

1   As the poet said:

2   'Nothing now can separate/The corn and tares compactly grown'*

1   They called Herod to come and see

2   Came in his state chariot

1   Very noisy

2   Needed its exhaust fixed

1   Don't we all?

2   In his groundsman's steps he trod

1   Where the weeds lay glinting

2   Weeds were in the very sod

1   Which was meant for sprinting

2   Herod said

1   Dandelions may be fine and dandy

2   But not in my track yard

1   Some enemy of fun has done this

2   A killjoy has sabotaged the site

1   Some Pharisaical anti-sports saboteur

2   Who wants us to run a straight moral race

1   And only have entertainment

2   When there isn't a vowel in the month

1   He's seeded the sown sods

2   With weedy seeds

    PAUSE

1   What could they do?

2   Chemical weedkiller had been banned

---

* 'One Foot in Eden', Edwin Muir (in *Gather the Fragments*, compiled by Alan Ecclestone, page 17)

1   So only bandits had weedkiller

2   Green said:

1   We can't dig up the lot

2   We shall have to do

1   What God does with people

2   He doesn't dig up the whole world

1   And start again

2   He lets the good and bad grow together

1   Poetically:

2   'Evil and good stand thick around

1   In fields of charity and sin'*

2   God doesn't wipe out the bad

1   But lets us grow together with those who are good

2   So let the grass and weeds grow together

1   Until they are full-grown

2   Then we can see to separate the good from the bad

1   And let's all hope

2   That when God calls harvest-time to the world

1   Sends his twelve men out to mow

2   Out to mow his meadow

1   He finds us all coming up daisies

2   Not dandelions

1   Scatter seeds, not weeds, as you walk through the greenhouse of life.

---

* Edwin Muir, op. cit.

Do as you would be dunned by

1	Break for a commercial
2	Normal service will resume shortly
1	Commercially
2	Every business needs capital
1	Like countries
2	Like Jerusalem
1	Now Isaac
2	A businessman in Nazareth
1	Isaac Bar-Carole
2	Needed capital to expand
1	Very big in the small chariot business
2	Man of good wheels
1	In the mini-cart world
2	One horse, one driver, one chassis, one seat
1	Slimline Taxis
2	Isaac owned the concessions
1	The franchises
2	In most of Palestine
1	Isaac planned to expand his territory
2	A new mini-cart franchise opportunity
1	Right down in the south
2	The south: for sun, sea, sand and se-
1	-cond homes

2   Casinos and nightclubs

1   Known as the Gaza Strip

2   Isaac needed capital

1   Been to two banks

2   Either side of the river

1   They lent him an ear

2   But no money

1   So he went to the capital

2   Jerusalem

1   City of commerce and religion

2   A powerful mixture

1   For converting the heathen

2   The music of the tills

1   The National Anthem

2   All the shops were playing it

1   Down a side street

2   Isaac saw a sign

1   International Bank – Merchants of Venice

2   Had a shy look inside

1   Knocked, and it opened to him

2   Smart receptionist

1   With a burly chassis

2   The minute he walked in the door

1   He could see it was a bank of distinction

2   Hey, big lender!

1   Lend a little pile to me

2 And indeed they did

1 The influence of affluence

2 Quickly sealed the deal

1 10 grand at 10 per cent for 10 months

2 Decadent

1 Out with a banker's draft

2 Cash in the wind

1 Bought some premises in Gaza

2 Bought more modern Mini wagons

1 And amphibious vehicles from Norway

2 Fjord Fiestas

1 *Something between a large bathing machine*

2 *And a very small second-class carriage**

1 Advertised the franchise

2 In the Bethlehem Star

1 Chariots of hire

2 Taxi franchise business on offer

1 You run the business

2 We provide the wagons

1 Drawn by horses

2 Painted by Stubbs

1 Who always put the art before the horse

PAUSE

2 Along came Simon

1 A half-time Rabbi

---

* *Iolanthe.* Gilbert & Sullivan

15

2	Simon Bar-Owner
1	Who spoke two languages
2	Good and bad
1	Thought taxis a devout institution
2	Invented for teaching other drivers modesty and humility
1	They agreed a rate for the franchise
2	And Simon opened for business
1	Under the name of Runaway Taxis*
2	Lower-cost hire
	PAUSE
1	Meanwhile
2	Back in Nazareth
1	Isaac
2	The big businessman
1	Began to diversify
2	In a small way
1	Bought up a small sandal factory
2	Everyone was wearing feet that year
1	Moved into financial services
2	Creative accounting for architects
1	Inventories for the infantry
2	Balance sheets for ballerinas
1	Capital letter deliveries
2	But expanded too quickly
1	And blew his opportunities

---

* A pun on a local business; adapt to your locality

2	The income tap suddenly turned off
1	Cash flow problems
2	Instead of drowning in ducats
1	He was like a duck in a drought
2	Put a cap on his overheads
1	Couldn't repay the 10 grand he'd been lent
2	Until next Ash Wednesday
1	So he grovelled to Jerusalem
2	Knocked on the bank door again
1	Which was opened to him again
2	He felt like a trespasser led into temptation
1	As he pleaded for time to repay
	PAUSE
2	Now the Manager
1	Of the Merchants of Venice
2	Although he ran a Porsche
1	The quality of his mercy was not strained
2	Forgave Isaac his trespassing
1	He forgave the debt
2	Freed him from his burden
1	And delivered Isaac from evil
2	Capital charity!
1	How God loves a cheerful giver!
2	But in Gaza
1	The franchise wasn't going well
2	Chill wind of change

1   Simon didn't know where the wind came from

2   But it went straight to his trouser pockets

1   Unseasonal rain turned the streets to mud

2   Chariot wheels clogged

1   Like the Egyptians

2   Better Dead than Red, see

1   Traffic chaos

2   The City Council cut taxis

1   And banned wagons

2   For Simon

1   Trade petered out

2   And he couldn't keep up payments to Isaac

1   Pleaded for time and mercy

2   But Isaac didn't give credit where it was due

1   Sent in a firm of debt-collectors

2   Dunn, Duncan and Dunitall, bailiffs and house clearance

1   The heavy squad

2   They stripped Simon of all he had

1   Not enough left to give him his daily bread

2   Isaac, free from his huge debt

1   Never let Simon free from the small debts

2   What would God say about that?

    LENGTHY PAUSE – then SLOW

1   I forgive all your debts as you forgive those who trespass against you.

The royal banquet

1   The King asked
The Queen, and
The Queen asked
The Diary-man:

2   'One requires a Royal Party
At the Dedication Feast.'

1   The Queen asked
The Diary-man,

2   The Diary-man
Said: 'Possibly,
We should go down to
The Temple

1   And
Check it with the priest.'

2   The Queen put
Her crown on

1   And then consulted
Caiaphas.

2   'Would a booze-up
Contravene
The Dietary Laws?'

1   Caiaphas
Said sleepily:

2   'You'd better tell
His Majesty

1   That many people nowadays

2   Like barbecues
Outdoors.'

1   The Queen said:

2   'Oh!'

1   And went to
His Majesty.

2   'Talking of the party for
The Royal Temple Feast,
Many people
Think that

1   Barbecues
Are nicer.

2   Would you like to try a little
Barbecue at least?'

1   The King said:

2   'Bother!'

1   And then he said:

2   'Oh, deary me!'

1   The King screamed:

2   'Who is he
to tell me what to do?
Nobody,'

1   He shouted,

2   'Could call me
A jolly man;

1   But I want
A jolly party

2   And I'm jolly
Going to!'

1   SO . . .

1   Job, Joel, Moishe and Mordecai,
all the royal mailing list

2   Got great gold invitations
nobody could be missed.

1   Great royal seal on the envelope
        made clear who was the host
2   Everyone who was anyone
        found the card in the post.

1   Job, Joel, Moishe and Mordecai,
        resurvupped on the next day.
    Small, plain, white bits of paper:
2   'Dear King, sorry to say . . .'
1   'Prayer Group meets every Tuesday;'
2   'Have to refuse with regret.'
1   'Too much to do;' 'Both got the flu;'
2   'Taking the cat to the vet.'

1   Jesse and brothers, handyman builders,
        Needed three tons of bricks
2   'We're going right down to the end of the town
        And can't be back by six.'
1   Nahum, Mazor and Saphoth, the farmers, said:
2   'Cows and sheep keep us up late.
    If you'll excuse an expression we use,
        Mucking out muck cannot wait.'

1   Jason, Heime, Manasseh and Malachi,
        Gents outfitters regal
2   Wrote 'Got a big job on; awful new cotton
        Won't go through the eye of our needle.'
1   James, Jacob, makers of ices
        Couldn't come though they were chosen.
    Busy with stocks of Damascus Choc Blocks;
2   Many were cold, few were frozen.

1   Job, Joel, Moishe and Mordecai,
        Asked to be all excused.
2   Not much fun at a party when
        All of the guests have refused.
1   The King said: 'They were the chosen;
        Here's what I now have in mind.
2   Go right down to the end of the town
        And bring everyone you can find.'

1 Fred, Ned, Betty and Gloria,
   All were brought to the feast.
2 The King then held an investiture;
   Bar-Mitzvah and Bar for the least.
1 The King he spoke to the people,
   'People,' he said, said he,
2 'You mustn't go wrong; always be strong;
   And keep consulting me.'

1 Job, Joel, Moishe and Mordecai,
   Haven't been heard of since.
2 The King said how he was sorry;
   So did the Queen and Prince.
1 The party's always open to all,
   All eternity too;
2 But if people refuse the kingdom's best booze
   Well, what can anyone do?

1 THEN . . .

1 Our Lord asked
   The Scribes, and
   The Scribes asked
   The Pharisees:

2 'Surely *this* is not Messiah
   Who will bring his Kingdom in?'

1 Our Lord asked
   His followers;

2 His followers
   Said, 'Certainly,
   If the Pharisees refuse you

1 We'll go and tell the world
   That
   The banquet can begin.'

2 Our Lord said

1 'Welcome;

2 You must welcome every
   Stranger.

1   Everyone is
Welcome
To share my bread and wine.

2   The kingdom
Is among you

1   It is party-time for ever
And in your joy
Remember

2   Everything you have
Is mine.'

1   SO . . .

1   James, James, Matthew, Matthias,
      Peter and Mark and John,
Took great care of the Gospel
      while they were passing it on.

2   'The party's always open to all;
      Jesus is King, that is true.
Will you decline the King's bread and wine?
      What are *you* going to do?'

Talents waxing and waning

1   Wotcher

2   Wotcher

1   Wotcher got?

2   Gotta lot

1   Lotta wot?

2   Lot of talent

1   You all have

2   Said Jesus

1   Gotta use what God gives you

2   Said Jesus

1   Like in that factory

2   He said

1   A candle factory

2   Known as 'Wicks and Wax'

1   Down in downtown Damascus

2   Candlemakers by appointment to the Scribes

1   But business was so bad

2   They expected to snuff it any day

1   Competition from the conservation freaks

2   Buying organic olive oil lamps

1   Fresh, fragrant and effective

2   No smoky smells or guttering stubs

1   And the Roman army

2 Weren't buying so many Roman candles.

1 The Head of Sales

2 Blamed the rigging of unfair trade winds

1 The Head of Wax Designs

2 Blamed the high cost of making fancy candles

1 Small wax models of Joel, Micah and Haggai

2 Making only minor profits

1 The Head Cashier

2 Blamed the high rate of VAT on vats

1 And an attack of auditors in the auditorium

2 So, the Head of 'Wicks and Wax'

1 The boss

2 Been in the business 30 years man and boy

1 Not necessarily in that order

2 Called the Heads to a meeting

1 To knock their heads together

2 And review the situation

1 Sat them all in low chairs

2 To see the bottom line

1 Told them all to use their talents

2 This downturn was just a pothole on the road to new business

1 He made a promise:

2 You've got two months;

1 I'll put money in

2 If you can get it out

1 So – sales budget, an extra £1500

2   (That's five talents in Judo-money)

1   Design budget, an extra £1000

2   (Three talents)

1   Cash and carry budget, £300

2   (One talent)

1   Put your talents to good use

2   Go forth and multiply

PAUSE

1   So the Head of Sales

2   With money to burn

1   Burnt his brain at both ends

2   Got an idea:

1   Every year every synagogue

2   Had fundraising Toe-Tingle services

1   Two-inch candles stuck in lemons

2   For charity

1   Lemon Aid

2   Those tiny candles

1   Could be sold in garden centres

2   All year round

1   With hyacinths and daffodils

2   Make your own light bulbs

1   He made a deal with Plants 'R' Us

2   Spent his £1500 on advertising

1   Jingles on BC Radio Galilee

2   Posters on mail boxes

1   T-shirts on female bodies

2   'Light up your indoor garden

1   With Wicks and Wax'

2   Orders rolled in

1   Sales rocketed

2   Like Roman candles

1   Soon got his money back

2   Doubled the investment

PAUSE

1   Meanwhile

2   The Head of Design

1   With £1000 to invest

2   Sketched out three new mouldings

1   For the bizarre bazaar gift trade:

2   Candles with handles

1   Called Noah Jugs

2   And his wife, Joan of Arc

1   Collect the set

2   All different;

1   Ambidextrous women soldiers

2   Called Madame Tussauds;

1   And a new line of candles with texts

2   'They wax fat and shine'

1   Jeremiah 5:28

2   'They shall burn and none shall quench them'

1   That's One Isaiah

2   Isaiah and Jeremiah

1   Made major profits

PAUSE

2   Meanwhile

1   The Head Cashier

2   A cautious soul

1   Afraid of losing his headship

2   And maybe his head

1   Had ideas

2   But didn't dare go out on a limb

1   Might fall out of his tree

2   So rejected the idea

1   Of recycling stubs

2   And calling them Two-Wax;

1   Likewise the idea

2   Of selling door-to-door from a cart

1   His life was of more value than many barrows;

2   Hid his talent in the safe

1   Under the discount coupons and the scroll vouchers

PAUSE

2   When the two months were up

1   They were back with the boss

2   Sales? £1500 of my money invested?

1   200 per cent profit and rising, sir

2   Well done that man. Have a promotion and a bonus

1   Design? You had £1000

2   250 per cent profit; returns still coming back, sir

1   Well done that man. Have a promotion and a bonus

2   Cashier? What about your £300?

1   Um . . .

2   Well?

1   Er . . .

2   What's the return?

1   Your money back. I was afraid of losing it, because I knew you to be a hard man, taking where you don't give and collecting what you haven't scattered. So I didn't dare use the talent, and I went and hid your money in the safe. Here it is – safe.

2   You stupid boy

1   Your talent was given for you to use, not to hide

2   You could have at least invested it

1   And shown interest in our future

2   You have cursed the darkness instead of lighting a candle

1   Now open your door and say after me: Goodbye.

2   Gotta use our gifts, then

1   Says Jesus

2   What you are given

1   Is given in trust

2   No good being faithful

1   And safe

2   You have to put your talent to use

1   Don't hide your candle under a snuffer

2   Just one's 'nuff to be going on with

1   Put your light on a pole

2   In your Father's house are many stanchions

1   You are the light of the world

2   So let your little light shine

Good neighbourhood

1	Nowadays
2	These days of Our Lord
1	*Anno Domini*
2	We're not supposed to say 'A.D.'
1	It's not P.C.
2	You have to say 'C.E.'
1	To be politically correct
2	And avoid offence.
1	Likewise
2	'B.C.'
1	Is blighted calendrically.
2	So the Jericho Gentlewomen's B.C.
1	Being very P.C.
2	Changed the 'B.C.'
1	And what was the Bicycling Club
2	Became the J.W.C.A.
1	The Jericho Women's Cycling Association
2	Kept the same motto:
1	'Go and do thou bike-ride'
2	Same President and Saddle-Person
1	Mrs Millicent Mason
2	The big wheel
1	And spokeslady
2	Who set a good example

1   Got her weekly shopping

2   By bicycle

1   From the Weight-Lose supermarket

2   Out of town

1   On the Jerusalem road

2   Uphill all the way

1   But downhill all the way home.

PAUSE

2   One day

1   Cycling home with her load

2   Millicent was whooshed

1   On a dangerous bend

2   By a speedy four-wheel drive car

1   A big 4 W.D.

2   Running on WD40

1   Knocked her over

2   She fell off

1   Fell over

2   Fell down

1   Spilt the beans

2   Split the peas

1   Spread the butter

2   Cracked the eggs

1   And cracked her head.

PAUSE

2   Luckily

1   She wasn't alone

2   The local curate

1   Was just passing in his three-wheeler Robin Unreliable

2   With its external combustion engine

1   And saw the accident.

2   Unluckily for Millicent

1   It was his day off

2   No plastic collar on

1   Short-change shirt

2   And fly-away trousers

1   And anyway

2   His life-cycle

1   Still had its trainer wheels fitted

2   He hadn't even started

1   His post-ordination essay

2   On the Church's Ministry of Healing

1   So he didn't stop to help

2   Had better things to do

1   And was hurrying to find out what they were.

       PAUSE

2   Nevertheless

1   Luckily

2   The Jericho Literary And Dramatic Intense Experience Society

1   Or J-LADIES for short

2   Were just coming out

1   After a rehearsal

2   Of the first all-female adaptation

1   Of Shakespeare's Queen Lear and MacElizabeth

2   They rushed to the scene

1   Scene one – Act NONE

2   Unluckily for Millicent

1   They prompted each other

2   Who should do what

1   Help her circulation –

2   – Turn her round

1   Loosen her stays –

2   – Get away!

1   Give her mouth to mouth –

2   – Button your lip!

1   Give her air –

2   – Blow that

1   Rub 'er legs –

2   – Got those

1   They clucked away like chickens on cocaine

2   But did nothing to help.

EXTENDED PAUSE

1   What this story needs now is a Good Samaritan

2   Problem

1   Two problems

2   Problem one:

1   A good Samaritan

2   Is an oxymoron

1   A contradiction in terms

2   We forget to remember

1   That when Jesus told his stories

2   Jews were wary of Samaria

1   Looked on Samaritans

2   Like something the cat had decided after all not to bring in.

1   So when Jesus made one a good neighbour

2   He wasn't being religiously correct

1   Not R.C.

2   Samaritans weren't good

1   Q.E.D.

2   Problem number two:

1   If Jesus told the story today

2   Who would be number three?

1   Who would be the big surprise rescuer?

2   *We're* all Christians

1   There's no one we hate

2   Or despise

1   We love everyone

2   Well, nearly everyone

1   We're all P.C.

2   If not R.C.

1   Very correct

2   So make up your own mind

1   Who do you look down on?

2   Rather not be seen with

1   Someone not exactly abhorrent

2   But very far from horrent

1   The people *over there*

2   We don't want over here

1   One of *them*

2   Not one of us

1   Make up your own mind

2   It's *your* story

      PAUSE

1   Let's say it was Henry

2   Any Henry

1   On a bike, of course

2   In Lycra shorts

1   Not a pretty sight

2   So much body-piercing

1   He looked like a colander

2   Came where Millicent was

1   Got out his mobile

2   Called the parable paramedics

1   Henry went with Millicent

2   To A & E

1   Where luckily

2   The doctors and nurses

1   Were not too busy playing doctors and nurses

2   Henry stayed with her

1   Down to X-ray on the trolley

2   Up to brain scan

1   Along to Path. Lab.

2   Then on to a ward

1   Deserves an award

2   Must be off his trolley

1   But wasn't that neighbourly?

2   He was kind

1   And he didn't have to be kind

2   Kind of odd, isn't it

1   How odd people turn out to be good

2   Everybody needs good neighbours

1   So when you fall off your bike

2   Pray there's a Henry on hand

1   And when you see a need

2   Be a good neighbour

1   Go and do a bike-ride

2   Go and do thou likewise

Nature's way

1   Late again

2   Blooming late

1   We're late bloomers

2   Time we were planted out

1   We're almost past it

2   Never really been near it

1   Time to sit on a bench

2   In the park

1   Enjoy the parks and gardens

2   Nature's way

     PAUSE

1   Had to park the car in the gardens today

2   Too many characters in the multi-storey

1   Too long for the short story

2   Lucky we have privileged parking

1   In the civic gardens

2   Guarded by Dennis

1   The park-keeper

2   Dennis will keep an eye

1   Needs to keep his eye

2   Or Dennis would be dense

1   Dennis runs the gardens and their denizens

2   Nature's way

1   The flowers know better than to do what they like

2	He lets them do what *he* likes
1	Inside the park gates
2	All plants inside the proper gates
1	Grow properly
2	Propagated in Fred's shed
1	Not Dennis' shed
2	Though Dennis has it now
1	Still called Fred's shed
2	In memory of the late Fred
1	King of Parks and Gardens
2	For 60 years immediately preceding his funeral
1	Started out from nothing
2	Became a legend in his own seedtime
1	Fred started gardening in a small way
2	Nature's way
1	Snow-white dwarf shrubs
2	Low-drangeas and Shetland peonies
1	And got the herbaceous habit
2	He was mustard in the job
1	Like a mustard seed in the Bible
2	Said Fred
1	As Jesus said
2	The kingdom starts with a small seed
1	And grows to cover the earth
2	So Fred's kingdom grew big and wonderful
1	From a small beginning

2   To a floral kingdom with many borders

1   Nature's way

2   Fred was a great gardener

1   Great sense of humus

2   And a great pray-er

1   He knew

2   'God who made him sees

1   That half a gardener's proper work

2   Is done upon his knees'*

1   Adam was a gardener

2   A dam' fine gardener

1   So Fred was in a good tradition

2   Jesus wasn't a gardener

1   But one morning Mary thought he was

2   And Jesus' kingdom has no borders

1   Starting from nothing

2   To spread and cover the earth

1   No wonder 'Satan trembles when he sees

2   The weakest saint upon his knees'†

PAUSE

1   Fred invented a new compost

2   Number one in 'is compost heap

1   You could hear it bubbling

2   Music to the ears

---

* Kipling, *The Glory of the Garden*
† Cowper, *Olney Hymns*

1   Put the organ in organic

2   Any plot treated with Fred's compost

1   Made poor soil grow more

2   Like yeast in dough

1   Like that yeast in the Bible

2   Said Fred

1   As Jesus said

2   Put a bit of good stuff

1   Into the ordinary

2   Like his Spirit in us

1   And his followers in the world

2   And faith rises up

1   Like bread in a basket

2   Fred's breed of compost

1   Aerated the soil

2   Nature's way

1   Made all the flowers

2   Jump out of their beds

1   Everything grew for Fred

2   Laurel and hardy annuals

1   Fine trees for shade

2   Where old crocks found rest

1   And the birds had their nest

2   In the shade of the cedar tree

1   Lavender and eight-foot lavatera

2   Need those in a park

1   Open green spaces

2   For those who wanted to be a lawn

1   Fred was awarded his park-keeper's hat

2   The peak of his ambition

PAUSE

1   Everyone knew Fred . . .

2   . . . When he grew old

1   He supervised Dennis

2   Dennis the apprentice

1   Green trainee

2   Made lots of mistakes

1   Gathered in the phlox by night

2   Saw the fuchsia in a crystal bowl

1   Thought ice-plants lived in the cold frame

2   Unfortunate incident of flower-bed wetting

1   But Fred said

2   Keep training him for another year

1   Be patient with his failures

2   You'll see him come good

1   Like that tree in the Bible

2   Said Fred

1   As Jesus said

2   If a fig tree has no fruit

1   Care for it and keep training it for another year

2   A second chance to come good

1   Be patient with its failures

2 God can make it come good

1 In nature's way

PAUSE

2 When Fred turned up his roots

1 Quietly in his own bed

2 In nature's way

1 His shed came under new auspices

2 Which kept the rain off

1 Now it's Dennis of Parks and Gardens

2 Thanking God for Fred

1 And for Jesus

2 Who taught us these three things

1 Our seedy faith can branch out everywhere

2 The yeast of the gospel makes a ferment of energy

1 God gives us seventy times seven second chances of coming good

2 Jesus is the king

1 Of our parks and gardens

2 He harks and pardons

1 It's God's nature's way

All on the loss of a coin

1   Hello

2   Hello

1   How do you find yourself today?

2   Look under the duvet and there I am

1   Turning up like a bad penny

2   Say denarius

1   Roman silver coin

2   With Caesar's head

1   Not a pretty sight

2   And Caesar's inscription

1   Proclaiming him a god

2   Which Jews didn't like

1   Naturally

2   But Jews had to have denarii

1   Ever since the census

2   To pay poll tax to the Romans

1   Had to pay in Caesar's currency

2   Twice a year

1   On pain of pain

2   Part of the cost of living

1   Cheaper than the cost of dying

     PAUSE

2   Now Mrs Miriam Behari

1   In Tiberias

2	Tried hard to hoard her silver denarii
1	For the taxman
2	Who gave no change out of Jewish change
1	So she saved the silver coins behind the clock
2	The water-clock
1	Invented by Vitruvius, from an Alexandrian idea
2	But Miriam Behari was fiscally challenged
1	Not exactly Mrs Money-Penny
2	And you never know when you're going to need to spend a penny
1	She sometimes lost the plot
2	Already lost two husbands
1	Never bothered to look for them
2	The latest Mr Behari
1	Was often away on business
2	Forty days delights
1	Ho hum
2	With a mistress in Gadara
1	The swine
2	Mrs B.
1	Poor soul
2	Found her own amusements
1	An eccentric circle of friends
2	In her house every day
1	Sharing the news
2	What had happened since yesterday
1	Reciting their autobiographies

2   No one better qualified

1   All tea and empathy

2   Sometimes played aqueducts

1   (Like bridge, only wetter)

2   And bi-directional Scrabble

1   Left to right Greek

2   Right to left Hebrew

1   Which has no vowels

2   Useful for triple-consonant scores

    PAUSE

1   One afternoon

2   Someone else came calling

1   Zak the Tax

2   Six-monthly call

1   Regular as All-Bran

2   Door-to-door collection

1   Turned up like a bad denarius

2   To collect the poll tax

1   Although a Gallup poll

2   Showed it was unpopular

1   All contributions resentfully given

2   Ungratefully received

1   And Zak the Tax

2   Was a man of few words

1   A Roget's Brontosaurus

2   Big and surly

1   Even his muscles had muscles

2   Looked as if he'd been poured into his clothes

1   And forgotten to say 'When'

2   A lived-in face

1   And owner-occupied body

PAUSE

2   Miriam Behari

1   Poor soul

2   Went for the coins

1   Fiduciary finangling

2   Looked behind the clock

1   Not a penny there

2   Lost for words

1   Lost for coins

2   Couldn't remember when she last had one

1   Arthritis of the head

2   Poor soul

1   To say no to Zak the Tax

2   Would be a red rag to a bully.

1   She got all her friends searching the house

2   While Zak stood fuming

1   Enough to clog the extractor fan

PAUSE

2   So, Mrs Levy

1   Wearing her best topless sleeves

2   Lost all dignity

1 Down the back of the sofa

2 So far as she could reach

1 Found only last year's free colour supplement to the Jerusalem Sunday Sport, commemorating the three-thousandth anniversary of the death of Abraham according to Usher and Scofield

2 And Mrs Adiv Kamari

1 A very large lady

2 With bad breath

1 Built-in space-maker

2 Looked in all the drawers

1 Found only old elastic

2 Then Mrs Hashish

1 Who had nothing to lose but her aitches

2 Leaving her just As Is

1 Lost her inhibitions

2 Turned out the beds

1 Only found dust mites

2 No widow's mites

1 Mrs Behari

2 Poor soul

1 Was in despair

2 Rent all her garments

1 A losing streaker

PAUSE

2 Then Mrs Grace Al-Rashid

1 Older and bolder

2 Ran upstairs

1	To the husband's wardrobe
2	Grace looked in all his pockets
1	Where moth and fluff doth corrupt
2	Found two silver denarii
1	There's a turn-up for the trousers!
2	Rejoicing!
1	Mrs Behari paid Zak the tax
2	You're amazing Grace
1	What once was lost has now been found
2	Grace has all our fears relieved
1	Must be like that in heaven
2	Whenever a bad penny turns up
1	God must rejoice
2	When any lost soul
1	Finds the price has been paid
2	And life turns from bronze to silver
1	God seeks us until we find him
2	And for every sinner who repents
1	There is joy in heaven
2	Angel voices ever singing
1	Round the throne of light
2	We know that God rejoices
1	And Heaven comes all found
2	– To coin a phrase

Pasture understanding

NOTE: As this piece developed, from a starting point in John 10:1-9, it seemed to take on a markedly less frivolous tone than my other dialogues. Perhaps the reason has something to do with the nature of John's Gospel, being as it is so much more profound and reflective than the synoptics. And of course his section on sheep and shepherds – such persistent Biblical imagery! – is a collection of parabolic sayings rather than 'simply told' parables. Still, this piece has its jokes, and should be performed *con brio*.

1   Nice in here, isn't it?

2   Lovely

1   If you don't mind [pink*]

2   Nice outside, too

1   Lovely

2   [If you don't mind the rain*]

1   Life is always lovely

2   Inside or out

1   Safer inside

2   In a church

1   Like sheep

2   In a sheepfold

1   A dangerous world outside

2   As our forebears told us

1   How many?

2   Two forebears

---

* Modify these lines according to the prevailing ambience, and the day's weather!

1	Makes eight
2	We're not bears, we're sheep
1	Two sheep
2	Among a lot of sheepish people
1	All Christians are sheep
2	According to the Bible
1	It's Christian teaching
2	Silly really
1	We're cleverer than sheep
2	We're not woolly-minded
1	Silly doctrine
2	Only for the birds
1	Ornitheology
2	Still, we are the Lord's people
1	And the sheep of his pasture
2	We do have to go in and out
1	In for rest
2	Safe in our pen
1	Lovely
2	We don't mind the smell
1	Sheep are nasally challenged
2	Better in than out
1	As the blackbird said to the worm
2	But we do have to go out
1	When the gate is open
2	When our shepherd comes

1   We know him

2   He knows us

1   Takes us out to pasture

2   Out to good feeding places

1   Better out than in

2   As the baptising bishop said to the burping baby

1   Pasture where sheep may safely graze

2   And blacks

1   And whites

2   So we are white sheep of the family

1   Lambs to the altar

2   And the shepherd stands at the gate

1   To guide us in and out

2   Lovely

     PAUSE

1   Real sheep have a folk memory

2   A flock memory

1   Like a rural myth

2   This remembered time

1   They remember it happening

2   But they remember it *now*

1   Which may mean it is happening *now*

2   It is always now to God

1   No time like the present

2   And the memory is this:

1   One day

2	A shepherd was hired

1	Who lowered the standards

2	A shepherd crook

1	The hired hand

2	Sloped off down the hill

1	Left the gate ajar

2	Left the silly sheep wondering what to do

1	A wet and windy day

2	Dull and overcast

1	Like King Lear acted by amateurs

2	And eight sheep

1	(That's the two forebears)

2	Two used ewes and two rams

1	Two tegs and two lambs

2	A disparate lot

1	Desperate for grass

2	Couldn't find their good pasture

1	Only fields of horses' doovers

2	They wandered away

1	Didn't know where they were

2	No gambolling in the fields

1	Gambolers anonymous

2	The hired shepherd didn't know *who* they were

1	And sadly

2	Seven fell over a cliff

1	Can't ignore gravity

2 It's serious stuff

1 And only one survived

2 A little lamb called Sean

1 And when the flock got back

2 Too late at night

1 For it to be late at night

2 The boundary between today and tomorrow

1 Between in and out

2 Life seemed different

1 Not so secure

2 The flock had suffered a loss

1 And everyone was affected

2 The farmer was furious

1 Jumped up and down

2 Like a kangaroo on a trampoline

1 He exploded with anger

2 They're still looking for the pieces

PAUSE

1 So now

2 The memory remains

1 Of the seven who were lost

2 Some sheep say

1 Better in than out

2 As the actress said to the sword-swallower

1 Best not to go out at all

2 Stay safe

1   But if we do that

2   We shan't eat

1   We shan't grow

2   We shan't be what we're meant to be

1   There are more important things than safety

2   Abundant life is outside

1   Only one thing to do

2   Trust the good shepherd

EXTENDED PAUSE

1   Mary had a little lamb

2   The little lamb was Jesus

1   Through him and in him

2   To him and with him

1   You find green pastures past your understanding

2   Lovely

Assize that fits all

1	By the way
2	Said the Rabbi
1	Teaching the Mosaic Law
2	To his new student intake
1	If you want to see law in action
2	Said the Rabbi to his rabbits
1	Look to the east
2	As you go past Nazareth
1	By the way of the bypass
2	On the outskirts
1	Hemmed in by the slip road
2	You catch sight of a three-cornered site
1	Flat and well-watered
2	Called East Trianglia
1	With a staggering stately home
2	East and west wings
1	Very flighty
2	Coloured mosaics
1	Illustrating Mosaic Law
2	All the signs of affluence
1	High quality drains
2	To minimise the influence of effluence
1	Rococo roundels and crenellated battlements
2	Swans in the lake

1 Kerb-crawling for crumbs

2 Even a sketchy drawbridge

1 *To separate the keep from the moats*

2 Certainly not jerry-built

1 By Jericho builders

2 But you might like to think

1 Said the Rabbi

2 That the Nazareth family firm

1 Joseph and Sons

2 Had several hands in it

1 Even my own hands

2 He said

1 When I was a builder

2 Before I changed my life

1 In the way I'm changing yours

2 I worked full-time for my father

1 And I still do

  PAUSE

2 And so

1 The Rabbi went on

2 Getting his second wind

1 More polite than the first one

2 In this house

1 Lives the local bigwig

2 Very big in wigs

1 His Honour Judge and High Priestliness David Solomon

2 Last in a long dotted line of judges

1 Separating right from wrong

2 Separating the weak from the strong

1 *To separate the sheep from the goats*

2 By the way of the Law of Moses

1 Which insists on mercy with justice

2 Thank God

1 And all her little angels

2 This Judge

1 For every case

2 Required the word of two or three witnesses

1 Where two or three were gathered together

2 He would get the gist from them

1 Cases of all sorts and sizes

2 Brief cases

1 Paternity suit cases

2 Even nut cases

1 Came to him by the way of judgement

2 Like, for instance:

1 The man who claimed his wife was poisoning his breakfast

2 Two witnesses agreed

1 He was always wan in the morning

2 Even at ten in the morning

1 The Judge

2 From whom no secrets were hidden

1 With the wisdom of Solomon

2 Diagnosed the need for a gluten-free diet

1 *To separate the wheat from the toast*

2 Next case:

1 A small farmer

2 Five-foot-two-and-a-half-acre

1 Kept a few chickens, ducks and geese

2 By the way of a hobby

1 To sell the eggs and the corpses

2 Brought to court his new neighbour

1 Who bred weasels and ferrets

2 And stoats – which are vermin in ermine

1 Pre-dating this case

2 The predatory animals

1 Treated his birds like chocolate penguins

2 Judge Solomon ruled

1 The neighbour was guilty of an offence

2 Must put up a fence

1 *To separate the geese from the stoats*

2 Next case:

1 There were three fishermen from Galilee

2 James and John

1 – Oh, and John Two

2 Needed a legal judgement

1 About their fishing rights

2 Since a pork exporter in Gadara

1 Brought in a huge container ship

2   Kept knotting their netting

1   Judge David said the big buoys

2   Must mark out a shipping lane

1   *To separate the ship from the boats*

2   Next case:

1   A public orator

2   After-dinner speeches a speciality

1   Suffering from plagiarism

2   Other speakers stealing his best jokes

1   Unlike Esau

2   Would not sell his copyright for a pair of partridges

1   Had now invented punctuation

2   (Which didn't exist in Greek or Hebrew)

1   The judge granted him a patent on inverted commas

2   *To separate the speech from the quotes*

1   Next case:

2   Couple suing for divorce

1   Tiny wife

2   Elegant, chic and petite

1   Large husband

2   Very angry

1   Enormously angry and grossly overweight

2   Something had got under his skin

1   Together with several friends

2   Their marital tiffs had turned tough

1   All to do with the food chain

2   And the padlock she'd put on it

1   To stop him eating so much

2   They wanted a divorce

1   *To separate the chic from the gross*

2   Next case:

1   Compensation claim against a laundry

2   For mixing up the items

1   *Failing to separate the sheets from the coats*

PAUSE

2   Now did it ever occur to you

1   Said the Rabbi

2   – Restoring discipline to his disciples –

1   That our God is asked for answers

2   And we ask God for judgements

1   All day every day

2   All night every night

1   And his justice is just and true

2   And always full of mercy

1   But did it ever occur to you

2   Asked the Rabbi

1   There may come a time

2   The end of your time

1   Or the end of all time

2   When our just God will ask you

1   Just what you did with your choices

2   And it just may be

1   In just the same way

2   At the end of each day

1   That sheep and goats are brought inside

2   And separated by species

1   You might be separated

2   Left and right

1   Home and away

2   Sheep and goats

1   By the way you have judged other people

2   And by the way you have judged what to do and say

1   Thank God

2   And all her little angels

1   Our God is merciful

Satisfactory child's play

1	Settle down, children
2	It's time for our story
1	A tale to satisfy every taste
2	So tuck in your tails
1	Sit up straight
2	Arms and hankies folded
1	Knees and eyes crossed
2	And listen carefully
1	– No, Hepzibah, you'll have to wait –
2	Some people are never satisfied
	PAUSE
1	In a primary school
2	Bright primary colours
1	Miss Jonquil Bloom
2	Primary teacher
1	In her secondary career
2	At age 47 going on 15
1	Had a colourful time
2	Her duty and her joy
1	Teaching the littlies
2	Satisfying job
1	Satisfying their random proclivities.
2	For today's story
1	She wanted the children all to be little bunnies

2   Not a popular idea

1   The children said

2   Don't like bunnies

1   Miriam said

2   *Our* bunnies keep hutching out little bunnies

1   We have lots of rabbit stew

2   Always more rabbits due

1   Prunella said

2   *Our* bunnies have bunfights

1   Don't like bunnies

2   Some people are never satisfied

1   So Miss Jonquil

2   With a quick change of plan and voice

1   Suggested the children all be little guinea-pigs

2   Not a popular idea

1   All complained and grumbled

2   Wayne said

1   My Granny says

2   Guinea-pigs cost a lot of money

1   Large deposits

2   And I don't understand why she says

1   Even half-price guinea-pigs still cost ten and sixpence

2   And Crispin said

1   Don't like guinea-pigs

2   They run up your trousers like ferrets

1   And tickle your fancy

2   The children all grumbled and mumbled

1   Jonquil Bloom's guinea-pig experiment

2   Stumbled at the first pigsty

1   God knows, his children of every age

2   Are hard to satisfy

1   Whether it's a funeral or four weddings

2   All God's griefs and all God's glories

1   Defer to our indifference

    PAUSE

2   Jonquil tried to clear her head

1   Back to its factory settings

2   And thought

1   I'll try changing today's story to be about fish

2   As long as I miss out the bit where their mother tells them to go and play outside and get some fresh air

1   Children, today's story is about fish

2   Powerful symbol, fish

1   You see odd fish placed in cars

2   *ICHTHUS* defined in the curvature of a line

1   And odd fish in church

2   Old trouts singing their soul out

1   Today children we'll all be fishes

2   – No, Hepzibah, don't put your head in the water bucket –

1   Miss Jonquil tried to settle the children down

2   With some fishy riddles

1   But they didn't know that the haddock said to the kipper

2   I've given up smoking

1   And they didn't know

2   That a skate is not a skate

1   When it's a skate bored

2   So she began her story:

1   Down by the river

2   In a little fishy pool

1   Swam two little fishes

2   And a mummy fishy too

1   – By the way . . .

2   This is a very sad story

1   Bring a lump to your groin and a tier to your seats

2   Well, the mummy bunny

1   . . . Er, *fishy*

2   The mummy fishy was making them party clothes

1   A fancy-*suit* party

2   A Post Office theme

1   Male costumes only

2   Fancy *dress* not allowed

1   But little fish Flopsy

2   Who hadn't changed his name since he was a bunny

1   Refused to wear his costume

2   Brown paper packaging tied up with string

1   Definitely NOT one of his favourite things

2   Some people are never satisfied

1   And the little fish called Wanda

2	Refused to wear her costume
1	Which was a pillowcase painted red like a pillar box
2	Because it said 'Eee-uRrrrr' all down the front
1	I've never looked so hideous
2	Oh yes you have
1	Now mummy fish was battered by their noise
2	Had red hair
1	And a ready temper
2	The only thing she enjoyed was argument
1	Wouldn't even eat food that agreed with her
2	But that does it
1	She said
2	You've plopped on every option
1	No costumes for you
2	Go naked to the party
1	Just the scales you stand up in
2	Your fancy-suit
1	Will have to be your birthday-suit
2	So she sent them off with no clothes on
1	– No, Hepzibah, it isn't rude
2	– No, please don't take all your clothes off, Hepzibah
1	– Because your birthday-suit needs ironing
2	Now children
1	Said Miss Jonquil
2	Go out to play, children
1	And all the boys are to play hopscotch if that's what the girls want
2	And all the girls are to play football if that's what the boys want
1	Rejoice in your choices

2   Because there's a sad lesson for us all

1   Said Miss Jonquil

2   You see what happens to children

1   In every generation

2   Who are never satisfied

1   Won't play God's games

2   Won't sympathise where there is sorrow

1   Or rejoice with the joyful

2   They are left naked.

1   Children who are not satisfied with anything offered

2   End up with nothing.

1   Bunnies don't have choices

2   And guinea-pigs

1   And fishes

2   Don't have choices

1   People have choices

2   In God's sight

1   We are all perverse and petulant children

2   If we reject one good thing

1   And reject the other good thing

2   If we're never satisfied

1   We end up with nothing

2   Walking naked in the world

1   And we must forgive God for offering us choices

2   As we pray to be forgiven our ungrateful hearts

Note: Echoes will of course be heard of Joyce Grenfell's Nursery School monologues. Sadly, she is remembered only for her comic genius, and not for all her other profoundly wise and holy writing. I remember her as much the nicest person I have worked (briefly) for.

Have aunts and you will receive

1	Good morning
2	Good afternoon
1	Good evening
2	A bad evening
1	Jesus once said
2	Which could only get worse
1	Before it got better
2	Jesus said.
	PAUSE
1	It went like this
2	Jesus said
1	On the 8.49 evening train
2	From Bristol Temple Meads Station*
1	In a first-class seat
2	On expenses
1	On his way home
2	Was Dan
1	Dan, the Quango man
2	There's thousands of them
1	Dan handed out lottery grants
2	Giving away money

---

* Or anywhere else which sounds mellifluous/mystical to you

1   It's a rotten job

2   But somebody's got to do it

1   Dan was used to it

2   And used to the travelling

1   On his own

2   Doesn't take two to quango

1   Settled on the 8.49

2   Back home to bed

1   Hoping for a railway drink

2   Pre-caffeinated coffee

1   And a railway meal

2   Don't ask . . .

     PAUSE

1   Time ticked on

2   But the train stood still

1   Half an hour passed

2   A voice was heard

1   We are sorry for the delay due to circumstances

2   The train now standing

1   Is expected to

2   And it did.

1   Later

2   A lot later

1   Another announcement

2   We regret that this train has been

1   And so it was

2	As if it had never been
1	And never would be
2	No more tonight
1	Please terminate here
2	Dan was hungry
1	And thirsty
2	No trolley
1	The Little Miss Muffet Buffet*
2	Tough – it was shut
1	All he had
2	Was his emergency laxative chocolate
1	Public enema number one
2	Where to go?
1	Suddenly thought of fruitcake
2	A pair of fruitcakes
1	Near relatives
2	Relatively near
1	The aged aunts
2	Kath and Carrie
1	Semi-detached twin spinsters
2	Could call on the aunts
1	If the aunts aren't in
2	Hotels would be a lottery his lottery money wouldn't pay for
1	Dan took a minicab
2	Promised to bring it back in the morning

* Preferred pronunciation here: Buff-it

1   Drove all round the houses

2   To relative suburbia

1   To the aged aunts

2   Where Aunt Kath said

1   Phew! Nephew!

2   Switched on her hearing aid

1   The deaf warmed up

2   Dan predicated his predicament

1   In simple words

2   Bed and bread

1   And Aunt Carrie

2   The practical one

1   Got a room ready

2   Cleaned under the spare bed

1   By kneeling down and sucking.

2   What Dan needed most

1   Was feeding and watering

2   Every aunt has tuna in the anagram

1   But Dan didn't like fish

2   Slippery customers

1   And Kath and Carrie weren't prepared for guests

2   Frugal living

1   No good solid food

2   Just a few lonely vitamins crying for succour

1   No currying favour

2   With foreign foods

1   Dan needed sugar, starch, grease and burnt crunchy bits

2   Have to try the neighbours

1   Even though it's late

2   They'll all be in bed

1   Have to knock them up when they're locked up

2   He's a nice man next door

1   Mends the panes in our windows

2   A nurofenestrator

1   At least he'll offer a good whisky

2   Co-ordinator for Neighbourhood Scotch

1   Kath and Carrie went round

2   The neighbours were fast asleep

1   Dead to the world

2   Carrie shouted through the letterbox

1   The dead were wakened by her call

2   Someone threw up a window

1   Caught it coming down

2   And shouted

1   We're all asleep

2   Go away in peace, to live and observe the law

1   In this time of night

2   Kath said

1   We're your neighbours

2   Dan's come

1   We're Dan's aunts

2   And the aunts aren't able

1   To make a meal for a male

2   We've got no loaves and only two small tins of fish

1   Can you give us tonight your daily bread?

2   Lights went on

1   Open door

2   Walk in

1   Walk in the light

2   What a welcome!

1   First, a stiff drink

2   Rum-atism

1   Then a grilled fillet steak

2   Cross-section of raw red onion

1   Microwave oven chips

2   Sweetcorn

1   Fried mushrooms

2   Fried tomatoes

1   Fried eggs

2   All oozing with fat

1   High supper rating

2   Dan was well full filled

1   Slept like a log

2   Snoring like a chainsaw

     PAUSE

1   SO

2   When you say your prayers

1   Remember Dan

2   And remember the neighbour's generosity

1   God is a cheerful giver

2   Just waiting to be asked

1   *And while we are all neighbours mutually*

2   *Holding each other up mutually*

1   *This only works*

2   *Because of the great hand from above*

1   *Supporting all the holding hands by their wrists.*

2   *There is no such thing as standing by ourselves*

1   *There is only being held up**

2   By God who holds us all

1   In his loving and giving arms

---

* Adapted from Franz Rosenzweig, *Letter to Ilse Hahn*

Porter and sack

1   In Judea

2   In the noughth century

1   (Though they didn't know it was)

2   At Netophah

1   Not too far from Bethlehem

2   Stood a small block of flats

1   Home to a flock of bats

2   And ten tenants

1   Making twenty in all

2   All under one penthouse

1   Where lived the owner

2   Joshua

1   A rich old bird

2   Rich beyond the dreams of aviaries

1   He designed the building

2   Broad at the bottom and bow-fronted

1   Modelled on his late wife

2   Joshua owned and managed all the flats

1   Service flats

2   Room service

1   Cleaning service

2   Valet service

1   Sabbath service

2   Housemaids on call

1   Meals by arrangement

2   With Feeder's Digest

1   Joshua employed all the staff

2   Including Mordecai

1   Hall Porter

2   Door-keeper

1   Whistler-up-of-taxis

2   Supremo of security

1   Always on duty

2   Often went without sleep all day

1   Live-in caretaker

2   Used to live in the city

1   In a square

2   Tessellated black and white

1   A chequered existence

2   In a flat on a windy corner

1   Suffered from flatulence

2   Preferred his new situation

1   *Better to be a doorkeeper in a house he could afford*

2   *Than to dwell where the rents were ungodliest*

1   Mordecai was now caretaker and porter

2   His job was to mind the doors

1   From his porter-cabin

2   A rhomboid cubicle in the lobby

1   Which was highly polished marble

2   Much like an indoor cemetery.

1   Mordecai the door-keeper knew all the tenants

2   Could tell you all about them

1   But of course he didn't

2   Position of trust

1   His lips were sealed

2   Behind a walrus moustache

1   He kept mum

2   And his mum kept him

1   As he often said

2   If it's not one thing it's your mother

1   So he watched the doors

2   And kept an eye on all the tenants

1   Counted them out

2   And watched them come in

1   Held the doors for ancient Mr and Mrs Zimmerman as they held each
       other up

2   All the gentlemen callers to sultry Miss Salome

1   Personal private dancing lessons ho ho ho

2   Supplied denarius coins for the meter

1   To Mr Gascoigne

2   Took away the empties

1   From Mr Sachs' wine-skin deliveries

2   From the tavern across the road

1   Wine-Bar Jonah

2   Where Mordecai took his lunch

1   Usually a pint of dark brown bitter beer

2 Known as porter

1 A delight of alcoholiness

2 And a posset of sack

1 The wine from Spine grine minely on the pline.

PAUSE

2 One day

1 Joshua

2 The boss

1 Back from shopping at BHS

2 The Bethlehem Healthfood Superstore

1 Slipped on the polished marble

2 Went synagogue over tabernacle

1 Nasty accident

2 Taken off to BHS

1 The Bethlehem Health Service

2 With a fracture to the tibia

1 And traction to the fibula.

2 In the flats

1 They put up a plaque

2 Joshua slipped here

1 Mordecai was left in charge

2 Responsible for all the staff

1 Chance to show his mettle

2 Copper-bottomed opportunity

1 To try managerialising

2 Turn his hand to anything

1	Especially the housemaids' knees
2	But with no one to manage him
1	Mordecai managed more time over the road
2	Drinking porter and sack
1	In a triumph of don't mind over it doesn't matter
2	Although he was mettlesome
1	He had mettle fatigue
2	So the dead candles in the candle-bra weren't changed
1	The rubbish wasn't put out for the Gehenna men
2	The central heating became peripheral
1	The cleaners were left in a power vacuum
2	And the valets went downhill
1	All the services started late and took too long
2	Sounds familiar
	PAUSE
1	Then came the day
2	When the boss came out of hospital
1	Unexpectedly
2	To find the fine mess his doorkeeper had made of things
1	No one to 'light up the fire, let the flame burn
2	Open the door, let Jesus return'*
1	Or Joshua
2	– The name's the same –
1	Joshua was furious
2	His voice like a crowbar inserted in the cracks of inefficiency

---

* Hymn: *Colours of Day*, Sue McLellan *et al*

1   Mordecai went white with fright

2   Looked like he'd been moon-bathing

1   He'd not been faithful to his trust

2   Or kept his mind on his duty

1   Not managed to manage the other servants

2   And Mordecai the porter

1   Lover of porter and sack

2   Got the sack

1   For a door-keeper musn't become unhinged

2   A watchman must stay wound up

1   A caretaker must give as much care as he takes

2   A porter is important

1   So if your master is away

2   Like Joshua

1   Or Jesus

2   Be diligent not dilatory or dilettante

1   As the Psalmist nearly said:

2   *Better to be a floor-sweeper under the penthouse and be bored*

1   *Than to swell with a sense of incompetence*

2   Stay awake, be alert lest he come and find you asleep

1   *Better to be a poor sleeper in a house of good order*

2   *Than rebel in pretentious ungodliness*

1   You do not know the hour

2   When your master will return

1   Blessed is the person who is found

2   Minding the doors

1   Caretaking of everyone

2   Lobbying for justice

1   Managing peaceably

2   Be a dutiful servant of the Lord

1   Not duty-empty

2   A servant of the kingdom must serve the other servants of the kingdom

A Gospel story:
Believing is seeing

1   The Hitch-Hiker's Guide to the Holy Land

2   Usually called The Bible

1   Says, Be sure to go to Jerusalem

2   For Harvest Festival

1   Everyone who should be there is there

2   So Jesus' brothers

1   That's James, Joseph, Simon and Judas (according to Matthew)

2   Hitch-hiked from Galilee

1   Up to Jerusalem

2   (That's down, on the map)

1   For the Wailing Wall Carnival

      PAUSE

2   But Jesus had read

1   The Rough Guide To Jerusalem

2   Usually called The Apocryphal Tabloids

1   Which says, if you're allergic to palm-waving

2   Manual or arboreal

1   If you don't like crowds

2   Packed in four to a suit

1   If you can't bear the noise

2   Of Hallelujah choruses

1   Best to wait 'til later.

2   So Jesus went later

1   On a Sabbath

2   Normal services had been resumed

1   In the Temple

2   Which Herod was re-building

1   As usual

2   Normal builders' delays

1   Blamed this time

2   On converting all the measurements

1   From Arabic to Roman.

2   In all the courtyards

1   And the sacred carparks

2   Where only the pigeon population was dropping

1   The only quiet place

2   Was the holy water pool

1   With its holy water feature

2   Courtesy of Herod's bosom friend

1   Gentle water music

2   Moses and Aaron a G-string

1   Gentle spouts and fountains

2   And funnels with holy lights

1   Jesus wandered around

2   Mingling with the sightseers

1   Until one man who couldn't see where he was going

2   Bumped into Jesus

1   Blind Bildad

2   Poor chap

1   A blind beggar

2   Poor beggar

1   Been blind from birth

2   But not for much longer

1   Because Jesus grabbed a handful of mud

2   Left by the builders

1   Said, Here's mud in your eye

2   And slapped it on Bildad

1   Urrgh!

2   Then spat on it and rubbed it in

1   Yuk!

2   Sent Bildad off to the holy water pool

1   To wash it off

2   Under the water feature

1   Which he did

2   And found he could see the light

1   At the end of the funnel

2   Nobody noticed

1   And Jesus wandered off

     PAUSE

2   When Bildad came back

1   Ten minutes later

2   For the first time in his life

1   He could see where he was going

2   The man born blind

1   Had no dots over his eyes

2   And wasn't bumping into things

1   So nobody noticed

2	Then somebody noticed
1	Couldn't believe his eyes
2	Surely this was the blind beggar
1	Now sight-seeing
2	Accused Bildad of fraud
1	Soliciting under false pretences
2	Wearing dark glasses
1	Just for a public spectacle
2	Others said, No, he really was blind
1	We've got a miracle here
2	A real sight for sore eyes
1	But who was Bildad's blind date?
2	He didn't know who dunnit
1	Hadn't seen Jesus, had he?
2	No sign of the miracle-man now
1	Everyone joined in the argument
2	Bildad's a crook
1	No, it's a wonder-cure
2	On the Sabbath too
1	Two offences in one
2	Riot, confusion and scuffles
1	In came the T.C.P.
2	What does that stand for?
1	They don't stand for anything
2	The whodunnit squad
1	The Temple Control Police
2	Every day's arrest day

1   Especially a Sabbath

2   Took Bildad in for questions

1   Without asking the audience

2   Only a fifty-fifty

1   Either a fraud

2   Or a miracle

1   Asked him about his sight

2   Foresight

1   And hindsight

2   He insisted he'd been blind

1   Until the mud-pie man splatted him

2   The police were baffled

1   Sent for his Mum

2   And his Dad

1   Sent a discourtesy car

2   To bring them in

1   But they said

2   He's our son all right

1   One of eight

2   We're people of breeding

1   He's always been blind

2   How do we know what happened?

1   He's a big lad

2   He can speak for himself

1   Meanwhile, back at the nick

2   The Police were quietly swearing

1   Obscene and not heard

2   Who was this rogue who made Bildad see

1   Hadn't he seen the notice

2   Pilgrims are not permitted to practise prestidigitation in the precincts

1   Sinners must be stopped

2   Better see who it is

1   See what he's up to

2   Is he doing it for money

1   Must be a prophet

2   If people believe in him

1   He'll get famous

2   Have his name up in candles

1   They had to let Bildad go

2   No charge

1   Absolutely free

2   Jesus found him, wandering around looking at everything

1   And Bildad came to see and believe that Jesus was Lord

     PAUSE

2   Believing is seeing then

1   That's right

2   St Augustine said

1   Faith is to believe, on the word of God, what we do not see

2   And its reward is to see and enjoy what we believe

1   Jesus says

2   Blessed are those who see in me things they never saw before

1   I see

2   Believing is seeing

Sources

These are the conventional names given to the stories in this collection, with the Gospel references.

1   The tares *Matthew 13:24-30*

2   The unmerciful servant *Matthew 18:23-35*

3   The wedding feast (banquet) *Matthew 22:1-10* and *parallel*

4   The talents *Matthew 25:14-30* and *parallel*

5   The good Samaritan *Luke 10:25-37*

6   The mustard seed, the leaven *Matthew 13:31-33* and the barren fig tree   *Luke 13:6-9* and *parallels*

7   The lost coin *Luke 15:8-10*

8   The good shepherd *John 10:1-9*

9   The great assize *Matthew 25:31-46*

10   The sulking children *Luke 7:31-32* and *parallel*

11   The importunate neighbour *Luke 11:5-8*

12   The door-keeper *Mark 13:33-37* and *parallel*

13   The man born blind *John 9*